in case of emergency press

We are proud to acknowledge the Traditional Owners of country throughout Australia and to recognise their continuing connection to land, waters, and culture. We pay our respects to their Elders.

We support recognition, reconciliation, and reparation.

Artful Women

Helen Cerne

in case of emergency press
https://icoe.com.au
Travancore, Victoria
Australia

Published by in case of emergency press 2023

Copyright © Helen Cerne 2023
All rights reserved. Without limiting the rights under copyright reserved above, no part of this publication may be reproduced, stored in or introduced into a database and retrieval system or transmitted in any form or any means (electronic, mechanical, photocopying, recording or otherwise) without the prior written permission of both the owner of copyright and the publishers.

ISBN: 978-0-6456382-7-1

Cover painting *Bridge at Warrandyte* by Lina Bryans.
The University of Melbourne Art Collection.
Gift of Dr Joseph Brown, 1982.
Used by permission.

Dedicated to Vanessa, Emily and Laura,
my artful girls

Table of Contents

Artful Selves 1
Self-portrait 3
Serious Black 4
Musing: Loving Partnerships.. 5
Organic Housekeeper 6
On Being Painted at 50 7
Questions to Fellow Artists 8
What's it like to have writer's block?..................................... 9
Supper 10

Artful Women 11
Another Way of Seeing 13
HD 15
To Dorothy Parker (1893-1967) 17
Found Subject 19
Ninth Street Artists... 23
Firecracker.. 25

Artistic Heterosexual Partnerships 27
Action Painters... 29
Snapshots 31
Frida and Diego.. 32
Marvel Claudel and Rodin 33
Equivalents?... 34
Patchwork Quilt... 35
Abstract Realist.. 37
Asunder.. 39
The Muses of Picasso and Dali 40

Heterosexual Writing Partnerships 43
Collaborator... 45
The Real Stuff 46
Existentialists 47
You Said 48
Mermaid Singing 49
Shifting Perspectives... 50

The Other Heidelberg School 51
Jane Sutherland (1853-1928) 53
Jane Price (1860-1948)... 54
Clara Southern (1860-1940) 55

The First Australian Woman Artist? 57
The First Seed 59
First Professional Female Artist? 60
I was First! 61
The First Australian Modernist? 62
The First Art Dynasty 63
First, An Artist 64

Lina Bryans (1909-2000) 65
The Babe was Wise 67
Landscape Quartet, 1971 69
Circles 70
Colour 72
Impulsive 73
Hearing Lina for the First Time 74
Describing Lina 75
Exhibitionists 76
Haiku: Lina's Landscapes 77
Gift 79
Yellow Portrait 81
Why am I obsessed with Lina? 82
Pantoum for Lina 83
Repast 85
Restoration 86
Sonnet: Lina's Loves 87
Despite 88
Shrinking Violet? 90
Who was the Judge? 91
Blind Date 92
Final Portrait Retrospective 1995 93
After Reading Kundera 94

Heartful Woman 95
Elsewhere 97
Rings 98
Transfusions 99
Cacophony 100
Time for Change: Villanelle 101
Equivocal 102
Still Life 103
Mourning Star 104

About the Author 107

Artful Selves

Self-portrait

a copy
about face
a positioning
a reflection
a mirror
and
yet
divided self, naked persona
object, snapshot representation
fresh meeting of two minds
becoming the subject or
performing between
liminal spaces
a perspective
embodiment
or perhaps off your face
an ego putting on a face
a construction, a mask
or losing face for yet
another raw identity
race gender class
dopplegangered
fragmented self
a shadow echo
disempowered
another me
she/her/it
I/me/it
she/you
her/me
they/we/them
other split selves
self-reflected subjects

Serious Black

Since sixteen, I've worn black.
I wear it to fake arty gravitas
with the cool in-crowd at bookshops,
gallery openings and soirees,
some still quote Sartre sipping chardonnays,
taking life so seriously that to smile is bad faith.
I wear black to pose in haute couture—
Chanel's iconic 'little black dress'.
How ironic to wear black to absorb
the bright ideas of others.

I should wear black to honour night,
'Hello darkness my old friend.'
Wear black for midnight yearning,
reflecting on the magic of moonlight,
paying homage to celestial creation.
To wear black would privilege nocturnal
inspiration acknowledging its power.
I should wear black to show humility
for the infinity of a stellar night sky
beyond my grasp or understanding.

Okay, I wear black because it's slimming.

Musing: Loving Partnerships

I want to write an ode to partnerships;
wait for the muse to descend to get
inspired then learn there are nine muses,
four for just poetry, yes, a quadruplet!

Erato to voice the days of fervent love,
when passionate lovers share an erotic duet.
Thalia for comic fun as aphrodisiac,
a witty verse of marital mirth, bit dry bit wet.
For epic sagas there's **Calliope** for conjugal
battles over budget or bedroom debt.
I need **Polyhymnia** on a wing and a prayer
to sing nuptial hymns too hard to forget.

If the four muses descend,
my poem's almost set—
desire, humour, courage, devotion—
a loving bliss quartet!

Organic Housekeeper

I am not a tidy woman,
my drawers overflow,
clothes escape for air,
they seem to grow.

I am a messy cook,
crockery everywhere,
cups morph into mugs,
plates breed bowls, I swear.

I am not a neat freak,
never been fastidious,
cutlery triples on the sink,
so many knives insidious?

I'm never spick and span
with greasy pots and pans,
that mutate on the stove
to gothic blackened clans.

I am not immaculate.
My linen press over full
of satin sheets with secrets,
pillow stories memorable.

I am not a neat person.
Daily my floordrobe rises,
around my bedroom I drop
boho op shop surprises.

I am never orderly…
house objects procreate,
expand, increase, sprout,
they must be animate!

On Being Painted at 50

Wary of my age
and your critical eye, I sit rigidly
and earnestly try
to look calm.

First afraid of what
you'll see, then
intrigued by some
truth of me,
time capsuled.

It is revealing
but more of you.
Is it my face?
Or the subtle, searching
view of an artist?

Questions to Fellow Artists

Some theorists say
art is a retrieval of loss,
what are we seeking?
Who has gone?

Some critics say
creating is restorative,
what is missing?
Who is lost?

Some artists say
we create to have new lives,
to experience other places.
A way to deal with loss?

Some philosophers say
absence and silence
speak louder than words.
Do we fill or feel the gaps?

What's it like to have writer's block?
It feels like you have swallowed a big large heavy paper-weight, it's blocking your creative ideas and especially your imaginary right brain and this feels like you could knock someone's block off, usually your own, because your zany inspiration is clogged and you are not in the zone or space for creating new tropes or themes or witty phrases so you get up and go for a walk around the block but like a defensive batsman you block all artistic notions, insights, witty dreams, dialogues, thickening plots plus rising climaxes with so clever endings, and twists that entertain and they're compelling but you just can't write them all down because you are a blockhead, a boring, dull, stolid, too insensitive hack who only thinks in dry sentence blocks, banalities, cliches that all you feel like doing is putting your so congested head on a great, big, bloody chopping block

Supper

caffeine manic
they wake at night
hungry for food
even raw flesh of
themselves

electric high
they make a meal
of what's there from
leftovers of domestic
blood

writers

Artful Women

Another Way of Seeing

Agnes Goodsir (1864-1939)

How could they keep me down
on the farm after I saw Paree?
I lived in the Rue de L'Odeon
in the Latin Quarter
with my muse and inspiration
'Cherry' who's on top
of all the fine portraits,
the rich, decorative studies
of women I ever painted.

Even commissioned to paint Mussolini!
Plus I painted Sunday Reed
then Mrs Leonard Quinn,
the portrait went missing.
Yes, well known in Europe
but back on the farm
seen only in regional galleries
or as a footnote
in Heide's hetero history.

Janet Cumbrae Stewart (1883-1960)

My pastels of beautiful women,
naked nubile girls
referenced traditions associated
with the feminine—
ballet, fairies, flowers, dolls,
nostalgia, china painting,
women in performance.
Male critics noted
my lack of 'eroticism'
as compared to the sexy masculine
validated vision of Lindsay.
They could not imagine
what a woman could feel
for other females,
could not conceive
the 'other' way of seeing or envisage
the transformative glamour of costume,
the cultural power of female identity,
nor the authentic gaze of a lesbian.

HD

Hilda Doolittle (1886-1961)

My initials as a girl were HD.
I signed them on class lists,
autograph books, in love hearts
for boys who didn't fancy me.

A young teacher, I was HD,
co-signed school cheques,
initialled school rolls,
signing off days in diaries.

I yearned to be a creative me,
a writer, poet or painter?
Someone who shapes meaning?
An artistic HD?

Then I read another HD,
 a woman who wrote poetry,
strong, sure, fresh imagery,
succinctly signed—just HD.

'Whirl your pointed pines, sea',
'sweet and salt on wind',
'lustres of olives', 'fire on
petal' wrote Imagist HD.

Poems of mythic Eurydice,
Cassandra, Sappho, Leda,
Helen, from the fresh perspective,
of a gifted feminist—HD.

Your wise words willed my
writing; with lines to live by:
'Let us not teach what
we have learned badly.'

Thank you,
simply signed,
another

HD
Helen Cerne (née Dougherty)

To Dorothy Parker (1893-1967)

Dorothy, witty writer, poet, activist,
your wry stories never out of print,
finally your ashes are laid to rest,
after being moved from here
to there for over fifty years.
Your famous one liners now
clichés everywhere:
'Men seldom make passes
at girls that wear glasses.'
Dorothy, dark humourist extraordinaire,
you wrote iconic lines with sarcastic flair;
She hurt herself 'sliding down a barrister.'
'Beauty is only skin deep but
ugly goes clean to the bone.'
'Serves me right for putting
all my eggs in the one bastard.'
Your pithy, caustic battles with the bottle:
'One more drink and I'll be under the host.'
Your clever word plays still throttle:
'I'd rather a bottle in front of me
than a frontal lobotomy.'
Your cynical, hard-won writing wisdom:
'Two most beautiful words… cheque enclosed.'
'I hate writing, I love having written.'
'Of course, I talk to myself. I like a good speaker,
and I appreciate an intelligent audience.'
'There's a hell of a distance
between wise-cracking and wit.
Wit has truth in it; wise-cracking
is calisthenics with words.'
A sad, tragi-comic, never a hypocrite,
you left your estate to Martin Luther King.

At last your ashes laid to rest
in a Bronx cemetery,
you had the last laugh,
with your self-chosen epitaph,
'Excuse my dust.'

Found Subject

Rosalie Gascoigne (1917-1999)

Late starter,
you were looking at the land,
while your husband, the astronomer,
was staring at the stars.
You loved the effect of light, air and space
on the long low landscape.
Bored, restless, a middle-aged mother
your visual hunger sent you scavenging
for found objects—wire, enamel jugs, wooden boxes,
galvanised tin, ironic bits and pieces.
Fossicking in tips you found your voice,
a patchwork vernacular in your assemblages—
casts offs and others' junk—patterned metaphors.
Ignoring local ridicule, 'Look at her!'
you dragged rubbish indoors,
discovered your artistic skill;
first in small box-like constructions
then large-scale installations.
Your *Scrub Country* on weathered wood
of old bottle crates evoked the land
as good as any painting.
You liked rusted worn things
which 'had the sun, had the rain, had life and vitality,'
which you cleverly juxtaposed
in fragmented elisions of found forms.
Your sublime *Monaro* with its lyrical golden
wooden strips sings with rural vision.
Then validation in 1985 at 67
you became the first female artist
to represent our nation at the Venice Biennale.

But was this as memorable as that day
two decades before when your husband
stopped looking through telescopes
and seeing your stuff,
your hand made tropes of the land,
said,
'You know, you're quite good with your bits of things.'

Louise Bourgeois (1911-2010)

A male reviewer wrote
this dismissive quote.
'Scary old Louise Bourgeois,
oh, don't pretend it's not true.'
Was it fear or hate which drove you?
Cages, knives, that huge spider at the Tate.
Sculptor, printer, writer, installation artist
of the century, you wrote
in your 'feather notes.'
'I am not what I look like.
I am what I do. I am my work.'
Your central motifs—caged rooms, spools of yarn,
hiding places—recycled lost childhood.
Fear or hate or psychological truths:
where genders blur;
where sexuality stirs the ambiguous
and menacing; where mirrors reflect
lucidity then darkness, where memories
cause pain, fear, walled-in joy, hate-love.
What did you recall?
'My early work is fear of falling.
How to fall without hurting yourself.
Later became the art of hanging in there.'
What about your latex fleshy materiality,
those egg-shaped protrusions, phallic imagery?
You deny this but with a smile.
Your *Femme Couteau* says it all,
your recurrent cells and lairs;
you cut the air with your female knife.

As a child your family restored antique tapestries.
You wrote, 'The needle repairs the damage;
it claims forgiveness.'
Your grandmother and mother,
socialist feminists, inspired you.

What did your view say of beauty?
Passive or active? You replied
you didn't want to be looked at,
but it was your duty to act.
'An artist must create beauty.'
Your complex art is a screen
for viewers to construct their own desire,
pure or obscene.
Your *Destruction of the Father*
works reject the patriarchal order by
shock, shattering stale complacency,
nightmares lurk in your interior life.
Unlike Freud you privilege female creativity,
secrets are shouted in your 'Three Towers.'
Your needle eye precision, pierces, penetrates,
provokes pain then perception…
the restorative power of an artist:
'I do, I undo and I redo.'
Scary old Louise?
You smile not true,
Oui, c'est vrai,
yes you say,
it's true.

Ninth Street Artists[1]

In postwar New York five artists arrived,
women whose skill and creative flair
dazzled the male abstract expressionist world.
You stood your ground, survived, thrived.

Lee Krasner (1908-1984)
Your *Self-portrait* 1938, said it all,
bold in blue, your stare says here I am,
your complex restless abstract inventions,
like *The Seasons*, fecund red, filled a wall.

Elaine de Kooning (1918-1989)
Known for your portraits and still-lifes
imbued with fluid colour movement
you blurred abstraction and representation.
Singular vision although Willem's wife.

Grace Hartigan (1922-2008)
Large scale sensuous abstracts that strike
the viewer, your *Ireland*'s swaths of colour
merge 'the vulgar and vital in American life.'
'No rules, must be free to paint anything I like.'

---

[1] Inspired by *Ninth Street Women*, Mary Gabriel, Black Bay Books, New York, 2018

Joan Mitchell (1925-1992)

Compositional rhythms, sweeping gestural art
inspired by nature, landscape and poetry,
your beautiful lyrical *Marge* in the NGV
sings with delicate colour from the heart.

Helen Frankenthaler (1928-2011)

In your pivotal *Mountains and Sea* 1952,
you invented the 'soak and stain' method,
paved the way for Colour Field painting.
You mastered abstract prints, woodcuts too.

Gifted artists you survived then thrived,
dazzled the male abstract world.
Women with moxie, skill, art flair.
Why didn't I know you'd arrived?

Firecracker

Shulamith Firestone (1945-2012)

What a surname! Firestone—
'a stone that withstands intense heat'.
Shulamith blazed with hot rage;
a firebrand, a fireball, a firestorm
of flaming words and action.

A combustible, fiery daughter,
her Orthodox Jewish father said
he'd kill her one day,
she flared back, 'I'll kill you first.'

Burning with anger,
she lit bonfires for radical feminism,
ignited the women's movement,
kindling three seminal feminist groups—
New York Radical Women,
Red Stockings, New York Radical Feminists.

Ablaze for more than equality,
Shulie burned for liberation,
gender freedom from oppression,
and control of female bodies.
Sparking an incendiary war,
a death/life struggle for women,
she torched the pyre of patriarchy.

Incandescent, her prose scorched:
'the personal is political';
birth is 'shitting a pumpkin';
'To be worshipped is not freedom';
'Power however evolved will not be
given up without a struggle';
'male' culture was and is parasitical

emotionally feeding on the strength
of women without reciprocity.'

She experienced the heterosexual Catch 22—
The Dialectic of Sex—
'Men are selfish, brutal, inconsiderate
and I wish I could find one.'

Sizzling with ideas,
Shulie's constant frizzle scalded
compromising women's groups;
reached boiling point with a lover
who unable to tame her radiant heat
extinguished fire with force.

Doused, disillusioned, schizophrenic,
Shulie painted, wrote stories,
slow burn *Airless Spaces*, the condition
where flames no longer flare.

Forgotten for decades
she died alone,
her burnt out body
not found for a week.

But...

flammable ideas smoulder
in the ashes of history.
Could such strong fervent views
still spark embers into fire?

Artistic Heterosexual Partnerships

Action Painters

Lee Krasner (1908-1984)
Jackson Pollock (1912 -1956)

Pollack-Krasner,
Krasner-Pollack,
all the critics wrote,
the hyphenated quote,
their modern art handcuff or bridle?
You were 'action widow' of Jack the Dripper.
Never idle, you lived for
three decades after him,
painting your own work,
protecting his legacy,
but you had artistic identity,
and integrity,
before and long after Pollock.
He was green when you met
in the New York Art scene,
both abstract expressionists.
Later in Springs, Long Island,
'action painters' of fraught energy—
your work caught tension and drama.
You in a bedroom while he had the big barn
and love and booze and mad rage
duelling-fuelling his fiery distractions
which burned away and enflamed you,
a middle-aging wife, who used the discarded stuff,
working them into collages fresh enough
to have new life—*Milkweed*.
Long before he died he'd stopped painting
dripping his life away with others,
speeding to that smash of splashed colour.
The year after his death,
you painted seventeen new works
as if out of breath in that barn where he'd been.

You became 'The Widow' of the art scene
perhaps by choice, known by his name—
but your strong expressive voice,
must have asked a thousand times:
'How do I crash myself out of his frame?'

Snapshots

Dora Maar (1907-1997)
Pablo Picasso (1881-1973)

In a Man Ray shot
Picasso first got a glimpse of you,
which he couldn't forget.
'I admire the utter fatality of objects,' you said,
photographing his head first.
Later he turned your camera at you.
Snapped, painted, or drew
his *Weeping Woman* a hundred times.
You were his lover, friend, supple muse,
agent provocateur, witness and doco maker.
From 1935-1945 a couple,
creating together during war, without then within.
Photojournalist, your chronicle of *Guernica*
has its place in modern art,
the start of picto-photographic process.
The first photo reportage of a work in progress?
Your lighting, framing and editing too,
clever montages, influenced his views.
Was peace too hard to handle? He left you
for a sleeping docile muse who would refuse
his aesthetic, nor confuse his own mythology—
himself as minotaur.
'I admire the utter fatality of objects' you said.
After you were dead your time-capsuled apartment,
full of *objets d'art* survived those raw times
when you were truly alive.
Becoming his object proved fatal.

Frida and Diego

Frida Kahlo (1907-1954)
Diego Rivera (1886-1957)

Mutual muses—
enough has been said about the elephant
and the dove—
his monumental murals, your small, stark visions—
paeans to politics, pain, passionate, piercing love.

Marvel Claudel and Rodin

Camille Claudel (1864-1943)
Auguste Rodin (1840-1917)

You fell under the master's spell,
working, sculpting, just as well,
for a few years his equal.

Then, a woman should not swell
with artful ego, pride and skill.
To sculpt, to create was to rebel.

Your sculptures were a marvel
but the male gaze didn't dwell
on art by a mademoiselle.

Your erotic visions did not sell
to Rodin's salon clientele.
His *Kiss* so fine, so sensual.

You sculpted *Medusa* just as well,
as his *Perseus* but he repelled
your desire and right to sell.

They expelled you to artistic hell—
creative silence your death knell,
thirty years in a lunatic cell,
Camille Claudel.

Equivalents?

Georgia O'Keeffe (1887-1986)
Alfred Stieglitz (1864-1946)

Did Stieglitz really say,
'At last a woman on paper!'
that day when he first saw your charcoals,
then exhibited them
at his 291 Gallery in New York?
What a find for him and for you,
an older man who believed in your fresh view,
inspiring you to leave the slog of teaching
hours and become the modernist artist
of stunning, revelatory flowers.
Not collaborators nevertheless
powerful influences on each other,
personally and professionally:
'He saw colours and shapes
different from those I'd seen
and so delicate that I began to notice more.'
After your marriage he photographed clouds, the moon,
even lightning he'd never snapped before.
Mutual influences show in your *Celebration*
as if in rhyme-rolling clouds, blue-white colours
echo in his *Equivalent* studies of the same time

But wiser than most wives you found a wider canvas
beyond influence, more space, spending long winters
away from him, finding in dry white bones
and relentless blue sky of the South West desert
symbolism and freedom.
After his death you lived there for forty years,
finding fame, ardent followers, critical acclaim.
First woman with a retrospective at MoMA.
Alone, you kept working into your nineties
with organic vision
and that room of your own
as big as the state of New Mexico.

Patchwork Quilt

Sonia Delaunay (1885-1979)
Robert Delaunay (1885-1941)

Most productive artistic exchange
of the twentieth century?
Dressed in bright yellow, blue and green,
strident juxtapositions of colour,
you both lit up the Parisian art scene.
Your shared theory of 'simultaneisme'
more lyrical than cubist,
symphony of shapes and shades, fine
use of structured colour in painting and design.
You shared the same aesthetic vision.
Who inspired who? Hard to know
how synergistic creativity does grow?
You were often dismissed for your 'craft'
while he made 'Art'. A perfect marriage?
No dominance or subordination?
Was this really shared creation?
Your first abstract creation, an important one,
the famous geometric quilt for a baby son.
You broke down barriers between art and life,
setting aside career to be the good wife,
applying his aesthetic to the decorative arts.
A gendered creative tradition,
you stopped painting.
Defection to that old chestnut?
'Men produce masterpieces
while women embellish homes.'
Responsible for the family's finances
your designs became in demand,
by cutting corners you became cutting edge.
Book covers, posters, cushions, rugs by hand,
modernist clothes stated identity.
'Her dress is a poem' the Dadaists wrote.

Your final decade full of collaborative note
yet not until '87 was a major show of your joint vision.
Caught in the middle of art and life
you said, 'I played second fiddle...
never put myself first until 1950!'
'Robert had brilliance, the flair of genius,
as for myself, I lived in greater depth.'
Sonia, the first woman to have an exhibition
at the Louvre, you knew the limitations
of painting, called it 'essentially static'.
Robert's in all books of modern art,
you sometimes, yet in this new century privileging craft—
the domestic and decorative at the heart of life—
you are at the conceptual centre.

Abstract Realist

Grace Crowley (1890-1979)
Ralph Balson (1890-1964)

Grace, you shocked your family
with red fingernails, red lipstick, and red ideas.
Avant-garde, always experimenting
with ultramodern style and content.
Never bored, you worked too well
with others here and abroad.
First Anne Dangar, then Rah Fizelle
then the love of your life Ralph Balson.
Together you made radical leaps into abstraction.
Exploring relationships of form and colour
you pushed the boundaries of Aus art
with bright geometric distractions.
Constructive paintings of linear rhythms,
you even signed his name on his work
as your script was neater!
For twenty-five years you painted together
in relative obscurity, undeterred,
saying, 'We built on each other.'
Poorly received by conservative debate,
and public dislike for abstracts,
fame, a retrospective came almost too late.
But
in the 1950s Balson retired
and
you bought a home at Mittagong
and
this became his most productive phase
and
you kept house and the garden
and
your output rapidly declined
and

you loved his 'wonderful paintings'
and
your 'poured' tea and a few fluid paintings like his
but
in one last drawing,
in one last brief return to figurative work,
in one last individual, ironic take—
you stand alone, your partner's abstracted,
and you called it,
Self Portrait with Garden Rake.

Asunder

Marina Abramovic (1946-
Ulay (Uwe Laysiepen 1943-2020)

You shared a birthday with him,
you under a red star, Ulay a swastika.
Together your dangerous rituals
of steeling and slapping each other
tested your physical limits of feeling.

Your bodies were performance fields—
his hitting then you reeling back
bashing and crashing into walls
until audience intervention
or exhaustion, stalled acts for healing.

But did your last collaboration
silence all dealing?
Walking from separate ends of the Great Wall
you met in the middle, said goodbye forever.
Hearts too empty or too hurt for feeling?

The Muses of Picasso and Dali

Picasso and Dali, passionate Spaniards,
born two decades apart,
child prodigies who could out paint
adults. They and their muses
changed modern art.

When Pablo Picasso was 23, he met
Fernande Olivier and so began
the rose period, then the cubist
style influenced by his women
whom he painted with élan.

When Salvador Dali was 25, he met
Gala, 36, married to Paul Éluard.
She was ten years older,
the lover of Max Ernst,
free woman of the avant-garde.

When Picasso was 31, he met a
new mistress, Eva Humbert, she
inspired his cubist works.
Woman with a Guitar, died
young. Cancer? Heart? TB?

Dali, impotent, preferred to watch
Gala, he idolised his wife,
accepting her young lovers
and strong sexual persona to
fuel their complex married life.

When Picasso was 36, he met
Olga Khokhlova, his ballerina wife,
who inspired his Neo-classical period.
They had a son then that itch began,
his roving eye, the restless life.

Dali said of Gala: 'I can measure
the slim columns of her pride, while
the tender and stubborn
banisters of her childhood, are
the divine stairways of her smile.'

When Picasso was 45, he
met Marie-Thérèse Walter, 17.
Voluptuous, simple, serene,
she inspired his sensuous nudes.
Soon pregnant and soon unseen.

Dali called Gala, Galuska, Gradiva, Oliva
for her oval face, 'She's my icon,
my eyes, my ears, my Lionette,
because when she's angry she roars
like the MGM lion.'

When Picasso was 53, he
met photographer Dora Maar, 25.
His 'weeping woman' whose photos
documented, influenced *Guernica*,
greatest painting in the war archive.

Dali painted Gala for decades,
her glowing face the feature
of melting dreams, the Madonna
figure in enigmatic works.
He said, 'If she dies I will eat her.'

When 61, Picasso met Francois Gilot 21,
a gifted painter and no doormat.
They had two children. She refused
to be his muse, with her strong free will
she left him and that was that!

Gala, cleverly marketed Dali.
His PR agent, made him famous, rich.
He bought her a Spanish castle,
could only visit with her permission.
Sold his art in ads, the new niche.

When Picasso was 71,
he met a potter, his second wife,
Jacqueline Roque, only 26.
She was his final adoring muse
didn't refuse his fading life.

Dali said he painted with Gala's blood,
her image seeps on liquid-rocks
She signed his name on his works.
Mother figure, he lost at sixteen?
Hence all the dissolving clocks?

Great modernist Picasso died 91,
famous for his erotic drive,
some of his muses suicided.
Books say they inspired his 'genius'
not martyrs who kept his art alive.

Seven years after Gala's death,
mad, demented Dali died at 85.
A dribbling wreck without her,
the archetype of his longing—
'muse of all muses' in overdrive.

Heterosexual Writing Partnerships

Collaborator

Colette (1873-1954)
Willy Henri Gauthier-Villars (1859-1931)

Was it selling out?
Was it about being a success,
having artistic clout?
Why collude with the enemy twice?
Or were you exploited?
Why the mute collaboration?
Appropriation by your older spouse
that user of talent, (what a louse!)
then by Nazi occupation.
Were you so young and green
you let him slip risqué bits into
fresh stories and claim authorship?
Were you duped into creative partnership?
After World War I you were made
a *Chevalier* of the *Legion D'Honneur*
So later why the back flip?

Or at seventeen when you first met
wily Willy,
you weren't so green,
learned quickly that fundamental lesson
of patriarchal oppression...
how to survive?

The Real Stuff

Questions for Nettie Palmer (1885-1964)
Vance Palmer (1885-1959)

You took on the role of Vance's researcher
became the hack writer of this co-operative team.
Brilliant, you wrote short pieces to make enough—
articles, criticism, reviews, editorials—
so he could write the real stuff:
'important literature, novels'.
You saw him as the writer
in the partnership.
Happy to be supportive,
the saintly wife and good mother,
you fostered others,
dismissed your ability,
gave to family your creative life.
What could you have written if you'd had a wife?

Existentialists

Simone de Beauvoir (1908-1986)
Jean Paul Sartre (1905-1980)

He was never your ex,
after you wrote *The Second Sex*
you always stressed his influence,
mutual indebtedness to each other.
But nevertheless
you flagged seminal existential ideas
in *She Came to Stay* in 1943
before his *Being and Nothingness*.
Where did your ideas begin
and his end?
Too hard to separate friends
sharing coffee, thoughts and beds.
You said one has to be
responsible for one's life,
not be 'made' a woman
nor become a wife.
But were you ever free
of Sartre's way with women?
Or ever see his 'bad faith' with you?

You Said

Ruth Park (1917-2010)
D'arcy Niland (1917-1967)

You shared 25 great years
of collaboration with D'arcy Niland.
You said, 'After a day's work we'd pin up pieces of prose
and each was free to borrow from the other.'
You said, 'We set sparks off one another.'
You said it was a team effort—
'we learned from each other'.
You said it was a long fruitful marriage,
a successful loving relationship.
But you were a mother raising kids
with little time to write.
You said D'Arcy got the desk
and room to work in,
while you wrote on 'the kitchen table,
the ironing board, the bed or your knees'.
You said it was an equal partnership...
Oh please!

Mermaid Singing

Charmian Clift (1923-1969)
George Johnston (1912-1970)

Was suicide your only option?
You wrote three novels together
High Valley, The Big Chariot, The Sponge Divers.
A successful creative partnership,
you went on some trip together
to those Greek Islands
'walked those paradise gardens'.
He was a fast, productive writer,
you slower and private.
You fed ideas to each other,
a fifty-fifty split.
You had beauty, warmth and wit.
He was descriptive, you, emotional details,
together you wrote like a dream
forging your own mythic trails...
or so it seems to readers.
Your voice sang in lyrical novels
but motherhood, domestica, his illness
and the green-eyed monster
drove you back to Australia
to suburbia and editorial columns.
Did you see this as artistic failure?
Did you miss, 'peeling a lotus'
and those halcyon days in Greece,
when the golden fleece still lay ahead?
No longer the 'looker' or his muse
couldn't you face a world with him dead?
You could have had another fling?
Or did you end it all
because your siren call,
your mermaid, stopped singing?

Shifting Perspectives

Helen Cerne (1947-
Serge Cerne (1946-2014)

I wrote half the novel with you,
I wrote in first person
but you chose to write in third
point of view to be objective.
After work I heard you writing
while I cooked the tea,
into the night you typed away,
while I cleared the sea of dishes,
helped children with homework.
We wrote separately each chapter,
our voices quite distinct.
I wanted no fusion,
no silencing of my voice,
no allusion of loss.
You wrote on Saturdays,
searched for witty tropes
and painted Sundays,
while I coped with bills, kids' ills
and the spilling over of domestica.
We finally finished our collaborative novel,
called it, *Shifting*[1],
then I wondered in the last chapter,
why was I writing in third person
and you were now in first?

---

[1] *Shifting*, Helen and Serge Cerne, Vulgar Press, Carlton, 2015

The Other Heidelberg School

Jane Sutherland (1853-1928)

I painted with the Heidelberg boys,
Roberts, McCubbin, Streeton,
part of the plein air movement.
They liked my art but not enough
to be in their influential 9x5 show.
My style was as fresh, as good,
as urgent, capturing the light,
atmosphere of our singular bush.
I painted women at work
in a domestic landscape:
The Mushroom Gatherers,
or solitary females
Girl in a Paddock,
or children, not lost,
McCubbin sentimental,
just kids paddling in *The Pool*
wagging school.

I never got the same money
though I sold.
The most requested was 21 pounds,
the bold blokes got threefold,
some 200 guineas or more,
What happened to Jane they ask?
My final brush or stroke
finished my art at fifty.
I died broke, restricted to home,
critics said my women are faceless.
I wonder why?

Jane Price (1860-1948)

No-one painted me
or remembers my art.
I minded the children,
of the male art elite,
a live-in governess
to the McCubbins
to make ends meet.
My subjects were
the moon and the stars,
light on fine landscapes
with a high horizon line—
gum blossomed Kallista
sparkling Sydney Heads,
Spring Clouds ever changing.
I worked with artists' societies
exhibited well, did sometimes sell.
A theosophist, followed Annie Besant,
now dismissed as a past fad
with all her spiritual cant.
Overlooked by the lads,
dead at 88, I wrote,
'Art is a matter of life and death
for the building of a nation,
Australia cannot do without it.'

Art history did without me,
but please never doubt,
my forgotten art
played its part.

Clara Southern (1860-1940)

They called me 'Panther'.
I was a tall, lithe girl,
some said a beauty,
with red fiery hair,
as if already aflame.
'The most prominent female artist
 in Melbourne' The Argus said.
I belonged to everything:
The Victorian Artists' Society,
The Lyceum Club, and that hub
'Women Painters and Sculptors'.
Yes, so bright they said
I blazed the combustible creation
of the 1890s burgeoning nation.
The first woman elected to the
Australian Artists Association,
sharing a studio and views
on life, land, love with the two Janes,
but not from their class.
The daughter of a saw miller
I too painted en plein air,
The Cabbage Patch
and women in the bush,
a hive of industry;
An Old Bee Farm and
A Country Wash House.

At 45, too old to conceive
I married a good man, a miner,
lived in Warrandyte,
nothing finer than Blythe Bank
where we settled on the north hill
overlooking the Yarra.
Evensong captured dusk's still spirit of place.

Around me gathered young painters,
a community space for artists.
Wealthy locals bought my works.
And then devastation…
The 1939 bush fires burnt most
of my life's work.
I died soon after.
A final irony,
I was cremated.
Ashes to ashes.

The First Australian Woman Artist?

The First Seed[1]

Emily Kame Kngwarreye (1910-1996)

I am and we are
my mother and my mother's mother
and my people's mothers
back to the Dreamtime.
I paint whole lot, that's all,
whole lot awelye (my Dreaming),
arlateye (pencil yam),
arkarrthe (mountain devil lizard)
ntange (grass seed)
tingu (dream time pup)
ankerre (emu)
intekwe (favourite food)
antnwerle (green bean) and
kame (yam seed)
That's what I paint whole lot. That's my name, Kame... seed.

We are the seed.

---

[1] Translated from language group Anmatyerre by Kathleen Petyarre

First Professional Female Artist?

Elizabeth Parsons (1831-1897)

'More than a Memory',
The title of my first retrospective,
but who remembers?
I was the first professional female artist
in Australia. I studied with JD Harding
at the French Barbizon school.
The first woman elected to
the Victorian Academy of Arts Council.
English, I emigrated
with the whole kit and caboodle,
morning sickness, a baby daughter,
two stepsons and a husband.
Often too busy to doodle
and juggle family emotions,
I struggled to remain an artist.
Yet I loved this new landscape
painted it with enthusiasm.
The critics found me disarming,
liked my charming watercolours
of the *Carlton Gardens* 1871
and *Melbourne University*,
but when I tackled the domain
of male artists, large landscapes
in oil, such as *St Kilda Jetty*,
I was swiftly discouraged from such toil.
'Her experiments are disappointing!'
The Argus wrote.
I took note persisting with painting
fresh seascapes and rural escapes
to form my vision.

My first retrospective exhibition?
Don't hold your breath!
Held in Geelong Gallery
a century after my death.
More than a memory?
If only, I wish.

I was First!

Ellis Rowan (1848-1922)
Elizabeth Parson, the first? Not likely!
It was me. The first full-time female painter
born in this country.
Diminutive, sweet-faced,
I was an intrepid traveller
in search of wild flowers.
On my adventures, encountered snakes,
spiders and crocodiles. Armed
with an umbrella and my composure
I was a humorous teller of bold tales,
My *A Flower Hunter in Queensland and* NZ
sold well. Forget about Louise Anne Meredith
or Georgiana McCrae...
mere painters of miniatures and journals
popular in their day maybe
but I braved jungles,
ventured to New Guinea, the Rockies
in search of birds and flowers,
had successful exhibitions
of my exquisite botanical paintings
that took meticulous hours.
Exacting in precise details,
I contributed to science as well,
as my eyes were too good for a start.
Von Mueller used my work
to classify species of unidentified plants
but no-one knew how to classify me!
Courageous, tough-minded,
a brave explorer of botany
yet physically a delicate bloom
pretty in my feminine gowns.
When visitors view my art
in the Ellis Rowan room
of The Australian Club at happy hour
they fail to see me...
the real wild flower.

The First Australian Modernist?

Norah Simpson (1895-1974)

My only known painting is
Studio Portrait, Chelsea. 1915.
A student with Datillo Rubbo
I left for London at 17,
still green, studied with Sickert
joined the Camden Town group
worked in Glasgow and Paris.
Saw works by Matisse, Picasso,
Gaugin, quite a coup!
In 1913 returned to Aus
with heady enthusiasm and
books, ideas and reproductions
influencing my old school and
Cossington Smith, de Maistre, Wakelin.
In that painting of 1915
you can see my modernist flair.
Thick bright paint. totemic carving,
behind a young girl with long hair
flushed with pinks and greens.
An English art book says of me:
'A lady of talent and magnetic personality.'
Then I vanished.
At 26 gave it all up,
life was different then,
controlled by powerful men.
I had a son to raise and wean.
Would I do it over again?
Choose between art and life?
Keep painting or become a wife?
My potential though can be seen,
in *Studio Portrait, Chelsea, 1915.*

The First Art Dynasty

Emma Minnie Boyd (1858-1936)

Biographers say,
'She had the money,
she had the time,
she had privilege
to create the first art dynasty in Australia.'
'She had a way with painting
but didn't quite have the range,' they say.
Never the sensation,
I left a legacy for a budding
family and nation.
My wealthy family had clout
then the money ran out
but not my dream to paint.

Today my progeny,
the first artistic clan,
now over four generations,
paint, make pottery, write, design,
with Arthur and me, it all began.

'Bankrolled a dynasty,' they say
but I was wise enough
to marry another artist
who shared my passion.
We just kept painting away
while younger members sampled
and witnessed our example
of creative family happiness.

First, An Artist

Ethel Carrick Fox (1872-1952)

I was an artist
known more as a wife,
then widow of Emmanuel Phillip Fox.
They say I faked his name on paintings.
I lived to paint
and live life as an artist
travelling foreign places
painting the vivid bright colours
of Arabian markets
and exotic cultural spaces.
I didn't want children
or to be tied down
with family obligations.
My Jewish-in-laws didn't take to me
Thought I'd spoiled Mannie's life.
I acquired no home,
nor many possessions,
just art and theosophy.
I lived at the Melbourne Lyceum Club
and the Mosman Theosophical headquarters.
On my death certificate
next to occupation
someone wrote 'home duties'.
Nothing else.
The final insult: home duties.

My time was yet to come...
In 1996 I became Australia's
highest priced woman artist
when my *French Flower Market*,
became the first painting by a female
to sell for over $100,000.

Lina Bryans (1909-2000)

The Babe was Wise

Lina Bryans (1909-2000) [1]
William 'Jock' Frater (1890-1974)

A review called you, 'Rare modern'.
Lina, agent of your own life,
a divorced mother with a child,
at 26 you'd ditched being a wife
when Frater saw your intuitive talent,
fuelled your creative fires for a decade.

Winsome, you liked gifted men and women
around you who could talk and think,
bought Darebin Pub, painted it pink.
Here, an arty hub to rival Heide,
lived and worked sharing views
but not the bills all paid by you.
Frater's portrait of you, *The Red Hat*
captures the elegant woman you were.
Your *The Babe is Wise* mirrored that
but with fresher gestural line.
You both painted modernist seascapes,
on field trips along the western coast.
NGV walls echo your fine connection,
who influenced who the most?
Superb hostess, you supported painters
and writers of note; discussing and reading
what they said or wrote.
Melbourne society loved your stylish ways,
your cultural forays into art and lit.
A natural 'haptic' artist,
you avoided emotional strife;
never victim with that clever wit,

---

[1] Gillian Forwood, *Rare Modern, Lina Bryans 1909-2000*. The Miegunyah Press, 2003

too wise to become another artist's wife,
you soon moved on to other loves,
kept that special flair for friendship,
especially with creative women.
Blessed with talent, looks, personality, health
you also had the sine qua non for acceptance
in conservative post-war Melbourne—
inherited wealth.

Landscape Quartet, 1971

Searching shadowed silence—
I find this singing painting
in NGV storage.
Lina studied music as a girl
and I can hear
rising notes, lyrical lines
evoking symphonic abstraction.
Over three decades
the modernist progress she made
from tentative tree preludes in
Flagstaff Gardens, 1937
to this tonal bush scape of
crescendoed harmony stirs me.
Strong verticals,
verdant thrusts, gestural rhythms
in horizontal running greens,
magenta, mauved scaled greys,
across four panels of dynamic growth—
a segue of sonorous notes
in movement and mood.
A harmonic masterpiece,
although screened
in muted darkness,
its fortissimo colours
outscore any 'maestro'
on gallery display.

Circles

Lina,
you were the only Australian woman artist
to gather around her
like minded artists and writers—
men and women—
the Darebin Circle.

Heide was different,
the Reeds were patrons
of satellite artists spinning
around the sun—John's modernist ideas,
and Sunday's heart.

Montsalvat had 'Genius' Jorgensen
hierarchical centrepiece
laying down the law about his greatness;
while others circled silently,
his women dutiful servants.

Around the potter's wheel.
the Boyds became a dynasty,
generations of artisans
married their peers,
a family ring of painters.

The Darebin circle were free,
liberal modernists in Melbourne;
a community of equals.
Art the central focus
rotating around itself.

Lina, never dizzy, you listened
to others spin art beliefs,
organised great parties
then sometimes orbited
off to the movies.

You watched others whirl,
you read spiralling writing;
you spun attentive support
full circle while creating
your pivotal paintings.

You were the only Australian woman artist,
the hub of a creative community
who didn't want to be
or need to be
the nub of attention.

Colour

Although out of sight
in cold off site gallery storage
your bright colours burn me.

I see your blazing strong
landscapes, portraits, still lifes
although out of sight.

The reds and mauve highlights
the vivid gold gash sunlight
your bright colours stun me.

I can smell striking seascape
feel bush writhing bluegreen
although out of sight.

A face glows with radiance—
the portrait's warm from within
your bright colours stir me.

Only one work hangs at NGV
the others all in darkness—
but off site out of sight
your bright colours blind me.

Impulsive

Living but dying in The Hotel Windsor,
your father asks for one last wish—
a baked rice pudding.
You catch a taxi,
rush back to Darebin
to make the dish.
Finished… you hail a passer-by
willing to drive you back to the city.
You rush to his room,
heart in mouth, pudding in hand.
Too late.

For the rest of your life
you can't understand
why he couldn't have lived
that extra hour.
You never make or eat
rice pudding again;
forgetting how that gestural rush,
that will to do something fresh,
left a man happy;
thinking of his youngest
and her best impulse to act.

Hearing Lina for the First Time

You apologise for forgetfulness
now you're eighty,
welcoming your blind
interviewer Barbara Blackman
by placing a pot of daphne on the table.
The sweet, strong fragrance,
a tangible gift, to smell the still life.
A good hostess, polite, reserved,
you share buttered scones and strawberry jam:
'Would you like another scone?'
'I would but I won't.'

I listen to your voice and
understand you better:
self-effacing, rather shy
I now know why you're
not more well-known.
Warm and wise you talk of art,
not your talent, seem surprised
when Barbara refers to your work.
Well-mannered and modest,
you deflect interest by your interest in others.
Would you like to talk about your work?
'I would but I wont.'

Describing Lina

Non-conformist,
creative, charismatic,
intuitive, bright artist,
used bold colours on canvas,
expressive, subjective:
'I paint how I feel.'

Spontaneous, sensuous,
attentive listener
impetuous, generous,
passionate, loyal friend,
impatient with fools—
a flight not fight persona.

A reader and thinker,
self-effacing, quietly spoken,
you had a low, well-articulated voice
with slow, thoughtful responses,
peppered with sudden asides
about family and friends.

About her first husband—
'He didn't have a lot up top.'
about Nettie's daughter—
'She went off her head.'
About her 'Mother'—'Terrified of kids,
afraid I'd leave mine with her.'

Elegant in photos,
stylish, well-groomed,
attractive, dignified.
Witty but never the wag,
in one hand a paint brush,
in the other a fag.

Exhibitionists

When I was nine my mother
encouraged me to write;
I showed her everything.
One day I wrote:
I want to be bold
and she said, 'I hope not, young lady.'
I meant I wanted to be brave,
fearless, not afraid to try anything.
She was afraid I'd make
a spectacle of myself.

Lina, your mother loved art.
Did she love you the artist
or prefer a ladylike daughter
who didn't put herself on show?
My granny would have called you a bolter,
my father a loose woman,
my mother would've said someone
who didn't do as she was told.
Lina, I call you free, independent,
my kind of bold.

Haiku: Lina's Landscapes

Music fills the air,
Eltham's alive with colour—
wattles are singing.[1]

                              A ribbon of blue
satin threads through verdant cloth
the Yarra River.[2]

Strong gum sentinels
stand guard over gold country,
Yackandandah hills.[3]

                         Greens, reds, yellows dance
trees and river waltzing—
Bridge at Warrandyte.[4]

Serene sea whispers,
vibrant gardens of Lorne call,
one bright red roof shouts.[5]

                             Dawn cacophony
white gestural daubs with red
streaks—clucking leghorns[6]

Abstract green brown daubs,
strong verticals plant design—
iconic gums—The Bush[7]

                              Red rock mouth dry,
pink, parched, ochred body
landscape's thirsty.[8]

---

[1] *Spring Landscape*, 1955, oil on canvas
[2] *The River*, 1947, oil on board
[3] *Gold Country*, 1943, oil on board
[4] *Bridge at Warrandyte*, 1959, oil on canvas board
[5] *Garden at Lorne*, 1943, oil on hardboard
[6] *Leghorns*, 1940, oil on board
[7] *The Bush 1*, 1965, oil on canvas
[8] *Waterhole*, 1973, oil on canvas on board

Tall gums shadow ride
horses fenced by sea and sky—
The Riding School Lorne.[1]

                                      Plum trees blossom white
                                      navy hills darken skyline,
                                            on horizon—spring.[2]

---

[1] *The Riding School*, Lorne, 1943, oil on hardboard
[2] *Plum Tree*, 1947, oil on composition board

Gift

I open the present—
a coffee table book
about Ian Fairweather.

By Murray Bail,
acclaimed novelist,
the revised 1981 edition.

I flip through quickly—
pleased to see a chapter:
'Melbourne and Lina Bryans'.

Delighted to find
Bail has acknowledged
your contributions.

Fairweather lived with you
at Darebin Bridge House
for over two years.

You'd bought his work,
championed him
before galleries did.

His abstract paintings
hung over your fireplace,
warming the kitchen.

Reclusive Fairweather
liked long walks with you
to Luna Park, the movies.

When he finally took off
you decided to sell Darebin house
and leave Frater.

Bail's bio moves on
another eleven chapters—
Lina's left far behind.

But on my second read
I see the revised dedication:
For Lina (1909-2000)

Yellow Portrait

Background is cadmium yellow—
strong sure line
embraces the subject,
Alex Jelinek—your partner—
architect at work.
Stark black diagonal
cleancuts design.
All spare lined minimalism,
side profile a new view,
sitter's no longer facing you.
Angles nuanced
in saffron space
your calling card 'colours'
discarded for linear grace.
Lightness and clarity meet,
fine gold weds dark line,
form, content marry;
partners merge into one—
designer-design

Why am I obsessed with Lina?

Your ability to express emotion
in vibrant art, give devotion
to others' work while refusing
the role of myth or muse.

The creative life you explored,
your refusal to be bored
or settle for less—
the mess of domesticity?

Your ability to cut all ties,
start again without the lies,
your refusal to remain a wife.
Seamless folding art into life.

Pantoum for Lina

You gave many paintings away
to friends, galleries, libraries,
saved some for a rainy day.
Would male artists give art for free?

To friends, galleries, libraries.
Were you such a soft touch?
Would male artists give art for free,
men charged twice as much?

Were you such a soft touch,
giving dazzling paintings away?
Men charged twice as much—
controlling art's state of play.

You gave dazzling paintings away,
for five guineas, for a song,
men controlled state of play,
your vibrant work was as strong.

For five guineas, for a song—
Frater charged more than twenty,
your vibrant work was as strong,
Vassilieff's 200 silenced plenty!

Frater charged more than twenty,
were higher fees too hard to sell?
Vassilief's ego, silenced plenty,
women did paint just as well.

Were higher fees too hard to sell,
critics loved your vivid art,
women did paint just as well,
you seldom sold at the start.

Critics loved your vivid art,
bold colours, your beacon cry,
you seldom sold at the start
far too modern for most to buy.

Bold colours your beacon cry,
you saved some for a rainy day?
Far too modern for most to buy
and far too good to give away.

Repast

Rich raw products of the earth
your landscapes feed me.
A feast for the senses,
resonant with loud
bold tangy ingredients—
delicious reds, corn yellows,
all mix in tasty bites.
Well-seasoned tones,
piquant highlights,
nothing bland.
Fresh flavours of
subtle, textured land
blend smoothly.
Your simmering,
stirring imagination
boils over from the source,
each course sustains,
restores, revives.
Zesty mint greens
redolent of memory—
a mother's roast—
you replenish me.

Restoration

You said you weren't outgoing
like Margaret, your big sister[1]
who you said had 'everything,
personality, looks, talent',
such a 'spark'.

You said you were quiet
while your sister was the life
of the party, could act, sing,
bring sunshine into a room,
'such a lark'.

You said she was the beauty,
everybody loved her spirit,
vivacious energy, lovely smile,
she was the artist who'd
'make her mark'.

You lived twice as long
as your only sister,
you restored her past so bright,
restored light to life
lost to the dark.

---

[1] Margaret Hallenstein (1908-1956)

Sonnet: Lina's Loves

Attractive, bright, Lina you wed too soon,
establishment wealth, rich family schemes—
Baynham Bryans, offered you silver spooned
status, but he forgot creative dreams.
You refused the moon but kept the son,
single, how to live on a small income?
Met Jock Frater, your fine art begun—
vibrant landscapes, portraits, then some
still lifes yet Lina you did move on,
singing your own modernist song.
Alex Jelinek, architect; one question—
your lifelong partner—when he came along,
did you see the artist in his young heart
or did he hear the heartbeat in your art?

Despite

Lina's friend, Ola Cohn (1892-1964)

Ola Cohn, 'a big flour bag of a woman,
healthy as bread, strong as millstone'.
The first Australian modernist
sculptor to carve freehand in stone.
She studied with Henry Moore
at RCA. After returning home
kept hammering, chiselling away
despite the conservative backlash
in 1930s Melbourne.

Cohn's finest work? Simple but monumental,
the seven-foot limestone,
the SA Pioneer Women's Memorial or
two sandstone figures for Hobart hospital,
or *Mother and Child* still in her garden.
Cohn used hard intractable material—
wood, marble, stone—using
a mason's hammer, a gouge, alone.

Her house and studio,
a converted coach house,
became a hub of artistic social activity
and an education centre,
she bequeathed to CAE.
Long term President of the MSWPS[1]
for 15 years she kept the peace
despite all of Pandora's factions
released after her death.

During the Great Depression
she kept carving *The Fairies Tree*
in the Fitzroy gardens,

---

[1] Melbourne Society of Women Painters and Sculptors

for the children of Victoria,
despite the heat, cold and rain,
despite bees, flies and mozzies,
despite dismissive taunts causing pain:
'Who done that?'
'Nobody done it... only a lady!'[1]

---

[1] Ola Cohn autobiography, *Me in the Making*, SLV, 1948

Shrinking Violet?

You said you were shy:
You were the pivotal Darebin force,
exhibited widely, had one woman shows,
dined, wined, supported
artists, writers, consorted
with Melbourne cultural elites.

You said you were reticent.
Your innovative lecture at Ballarat,
exemplified art with ideas.
You arrived in a caravan full
of others' works, spoke with élan.
'The most stimulating talk ever given!'

You said you were timid.
In France, at a Cézanne display
you asked, 'Êtes-vous Monsieur Picasso?'
undaunted by his fame,
Picasso then asked your name,
inviting you to his next show.

You said you were withdrawn.
Artistic director of Moomba book fairs,
long term member of MSWPS,
sat on art committees,
a Tribute funds secretary,
organised exhibitions at NGV.

You said you lacked confidence.
Walked out of an early marriage,
threw Jock down the stairs,
left the farmer on the farm,
attracted admirers, disarmed
a man fifteen years your junior.

You had strong will to do or die,
if only you hadn't been so shy.

Who was the Judge?

Crouch Prize 1966

Your *Embedded Rocks*
won the important Crouch Prize,
with images of raw rock forms
almost abstraction.

On a newspaper clipping
I read your handwritten
understated reaction asking,
'Who was the judge?'
You deserved the accolade,
almost three decades
after you started painting.
The 'impartial' judge,
Jock Frater, gave you the prize.
without a grudge.

Yet you ponder
was Jock mesmerised
by you or your art
even though you threw him
out of your heart
twenty years before?

Blind Date

Expectant as a giddy girl
I can't wait to meet you.
Will you be what I imagine?
I'm so excited.

They say you're attractive,
mature, sensible,
good head on your shoulders.
Will I be delighted?

I see you first alone.
Note your strong striking
profile looking straight ahead
waiting to be united.

At last we meet,
I stare into non-seeing eyes,
fine earthenware head.
Long unseen now sighted.

Final Portrait Retrospective 1995[1]

On the Ian Potter gallery walls
I meet Lina's friends and loves—
Nina Christesen's luminous looks,
three portraits of Adrian Lawlor,
Nettie Palmer and her many books,
Allan Marshall not jumping puddles,
Corporal Frater, Jock's son,
Jean Campbell in her jaunty hats,
Lina's cousin, NZ poet Charles Brasch,
Guelda Pyke, fellow artist, and that's
Shorty Lee, Fairweather's chess player,
Rosa Ribush, warm, winsome,
Lina's partner, Alex Jelenik, the stayer,
plus her handsome son Edward,
the face of ABC TV news
and then some...

Painted in oils that last,
they all look warmly at Lina
and me with their steadfast gaze
and through her eyes
and theirs, I see the moment
more present than past.
Not impersonal, objective portraits
dated by time and style,
enduring fresh faces,
contemporary portraits
that still beguile.

---

[1] *The Babe is Wise: Lina Bryans and her Portraits*, 1995, Ian Potter Gallery, University of Melbourne.

After Reading Kundera

Lina, nearly ninety, you said
after reading *Immortality*
Kundera was speaking to you.
The story begins with
an old woman's wave,
a spontaneous goodbye.
The protagonist Agnes,
sincere and genuine,
lies down on the grass,
forgetting the self,
to lose herself.
Being 'without a self'
to her is happiness.
Kundera writes:
'What is unbearable in life
is not being but having to be one's self.'

Lina, after you stopped painting,
did you, like Agnes,
start to subtract from yourself
everything exterior, superficial,
borrowed, artificial,
until your inner essence;
your light faded into shadow,
and all that was left
was that last authentic gesture—
a modest, warm,
accepting
nod?

Heartful Woman

Elsewhere

I watch you when absorbed,
thinking, sketching, painting,
so lost in landscape,
you're not in any space
I share.

You sketch me when I'm unaware
thinking, drafting, writing;
I'm so deep in thought
I'm not in any state
to be seen.

Rings

I threw my ring at you
walking home in darkness.
We heard it fall on the path,
its golden circle rolled
along the gutter,
lost in the void of night.

With a torch we searched,
me crawling on the black road,
saying sorry, I didn't mean it,
you laughing at my temper,
said it's just a gilded symbol,
a thing, a ring, not love.

You found its diamond
glowing in the flashlight.
I promised to never take it off,
come bright day or dark night.
You said never throw anything
again, unless it's a party!

Then you threw your arms
around me, encircling my life,
you fitted me well. I never lost
your gold again until that last night
when you rolled into that darkness
where no torch could find you.

Transfusions

An Italian friend brings me
a bag of plums.
I'm a raw, new widow
bleeding inside after
nearly fifty years wed.
I suck ruby red juice—
incarnadined.

A writing friend takes me to
botanical gardens,
we don't talk,
walk past exotic flora,
stop at one blood-red bloom
remembering—
in silence.

An old friend
takes me to a concert,
the symphonic music
boosts my being—
lifeblood that revives—
making me
more sanguine.

Another widow sends me
her poems of grieving,
her words say what I'm feeling
what I need to read—
poetry that is healing,
bitter/sweet. It's titled
Blood Plums.[1]

---

[1] Lorraine McGuigan, *Blood Plums*, Walleah Press, Hobart

Cacophony

Silence is deafening,
I thought a cliché,
but in self isolation,
in quietude and stillness,
in the shock of nil voices
that normally distract
me from myself,
I hear loud decibels
in the dead quiet
blast of separation,
the thunderclap of
distance from family,
the clamour of absent kids.
A widow's roar
echoes, reverberates.
In empty rooms of solitude,
some days scream loss.

Time for Change: Villanelle

She can hear his footsteps down the hallway,
hear his cool jazz piano loud and clear,
she doesn't tell others, knows what they'll say.

It's been years, they'll say, time for a new day.
Perhaps they're right though she senses him near.
She can hear his footsteps down the hallway

where his vivid art shouts on bright display:
'Not going anywhere, staying right here.'
She doesn't tell others, knows what they'll say.

At meals she tells him news about her day—
funny ups or downs, sometimes aching fear.
She can hear his footsteps down the hallway.

'Love is not finite, it does not decay,'
she can hear him toasting with a cold beer,
she doesn't tell others, knows what they'll say.

Is there a time to move on from sad days,
to leave behind the loss of loving years?
She can hear his footsteps down the hallway,
she doesn't tell others, knows what they'll say.

Equivocal

When Dad suicided after years of depression,
I dreamed he was free, running barefoot through
bright green grass, laughing with me when I was six.
I woke at peace.

When Mum died, day before I could bring her home,
I dreamed I was eight, watching her dressing to go out,
wanting, wishing to stay up late, always be with her.
I woke warm.

When my fun brother died from a burst aneurysm
I dreamed we were kids riding down back lanes,
he joked, chortling, he wasn't gone, 'just hiding'.
I woke smiling.

When my sister-in law became a sad shadow
from cancer, I dreamed she was our golden
bridesmaid again, a shining spring flower.
I woke in sunlight.

When my husband died after five months ill,
I dreamt my worst fear, 'But see,' he said,
'it's only a bad dream,' then the clock alarmed me.
I woke in darkness.

Last night I dreamed of full family days,
the happy-sad, must have days of life and loss,
the pull of Eros, the push of Thanatos.
I woke more or less with joy.

Still Life

an artist doesn't die
their work still speaks
to those left behind
from galleries and family
living rooms

when I visit friends' houses
and our kids' homes
there you are on the wall
Fauvist bright cheering me up

no end

Mourning Star

She
She saw
She saw him
She saw him painting
She saw him painting her
She saw him painting her vividly
She saw him painting her vividly yesterday
She saw him painting her vividly yesterday morning
She saw him painting her vividly yesterday morning, smiling
She saw him painting her vividly yesterday morning, smiling eyes
She saw him painting her vividly yesterday morning, smiling eyes still
She saw him painting her vividly yesterday morning, smiling eyes still creating
She saw him painting her vividly yesterday morning smiling eyes still
She saw him painting her vividly yesterday morning smiling eyes
She saw him painting her vividly yesterday morning smiling
She saw him painting her vividly yesterday morning
She saw him painting her vividly yesterday
She saw him painting her vividly
She saw him painting her
She saw him painting
She saw him
She saw
She

About the Author

Helen meets Lina, sculpture by Ola Cohn in NGV storage. See Blind Date page 92

Helen Cerne is a Melbourne writer who has published four books: a co-written local school history, *Vision becomes Reality*, a poetry, short story collection, *Just Heart Work*, a novel about creative teaching, *Those who Can't*, and a collaborative memoir written with her husband, Serge, *Shifting*.

Interested in visual arts, especially women artists, Helen's PhD, *Circling Lina*, explored the life and art of Lina Bryans, which alternated with her own personal creative narrative. Helen is the co-ordinator of *Western Union Writers*, a long-running Melbourne writing group. For many years she taught creative writing at Victoria University and is an ongoing judge of poetry and short story awards for the *Willy Lit Festival*.

Acknowledgements

First, I want to acknowledge artful women creating today, those remembered and celebrated and those who have been forgotten or ignored by history. This poetry collection pays tribute to some women artists whose influential ideas, art and challenging life circumstances should be better known.

The Lina Bryans poems were written as part of my PhD, *Circling Lina* to accompany the alternate memoir. With gratitude, I acknowledge my wonderful Victoria University supervisors, Barbara Brook and Enza Gandolfo. I would like to thank *Western Union Writers* for their encouraging, constructive feedback for my writing for over three decades. A special thank you to my post-grad writers' group, Scribes, for their friendship, reading interest and encouragement over many years; Enza Gandolfo, Sue Holmes, Bronwen Hickman, Margaret Campbell.

I would like to thank my talented friends whose sharing of ideas and fine expressive work mean much to me: Judy Keating, Janet Brown, Janet Howie, Vicki McGuire, Garth Madsen, Chris Ringrose.

For my brother, Ian, a natural artist, thanks for a childhood surrounded by vivid drawings and to his family thanks for your affirmation.

With love and appreciation, I would like to thank my special family, Vanessa, Mark, and Jenny for their supportive interest and insightful conversations. For Emily and Laura, I am very grateful for their expressive gifts.

And a heartfelt thanks to Serge for fifty years of inspiring creative example.

Cover painting *Bridge at Warrandyte* by Lina Bryans.
The University of Melbourne Art Collection. Gift of Dr Joseph Brown, 1982.
Used by permission.

Publishing history

'Self-portrait', *Offset*, No 11, Offset Press, Victoria University

'Self-portraits: the first Australian woman painter?' and 'The Other Heidelberg School', internet journal, *Journal of Politics and Culture*

'Found Subject', 'Questions to second persons: heterosexual collaborative writers', 'Second person as subject, snapshot-Dora Marr and Pablo Picasso', 'Patchwork quilt-Robert and Sonia Delaunay', 'Action painters, Krasner and Pollock', 'A wider canvas, Georgia O'Keeffe and Alfred Stieglitz', 'The babe is wise', Jean Campbell', 'A villanelle for Lina Bryans, 1909-2000', and 'Circles' in *Hecate* journal.

'Lina Bryans: the babe was wise', and 'Blood Plums' in *Poetry Monash*

'Equivocal', in *Joy in the Morning*, Poetica Christi Press, 2020

'Asunder' and 'Frida and Diego' *Western Reunion*, 30th anniversary Western Union Writers anthology, 2015

Awards

'Heterosexual Artistic Collaborations' won the Brimbank Festival Poetry Prize, 2009